Watching Heather Bloom

Watching Heather Bloom

Janet McKenzie Prince

Burley Creek Studio

ISBN 0-9667286-2-9
Library of Congress Catalog Card Number 99-95434

Publisher Order Number 99022PRI

Published by Burley Creek Studio, Annapolis, Maryland
Printed by United Book Press, Inc., Baltimore, Maryland

Cover & book design by Janet Prince
All cover and inside photos by Burley Creek Studio

For information, please contact Burley Creek Studio
P.O. Box 1987, Annapolis, Maryland 21401
phone: 410-212-3355 or 410-757-4455
fax: 410-757-5335, brlycrk @ aol.com.

To Maggie
whose lifelong love for animals
spilled over into the next generation
and flows far beyond.

Marjorie (Maggie) McKenzie Davis is a wildlife specialist in Northern California. She is the founder and director of Wildlife Fawn Rescue, a nonprofit wildlife rescue facility high in the hills of Kenwood. She is the author of a book that I published last year: *Leap to Freedom*, a compelling journey into the world of wildlife rescue. She's also my mom.

Each year, as she has done for more than a decade, Maggie rescues approximately 100 injured or orphaned fawns, tends to their needs, then sets them free once they can survive on their own. She is on call 24 hours a day and performs the rescues by herself. Considering her petite stature — 5'2" and just barely 100 pounds — her acts of heroism are amazing. Even more amazing is the fact that she is 79 years old and has no plans to slow down. She's my role model, and an example for us all who try to make this world a better place for the animals.

Acknowledgment

It is because of the good work of Wendy Opel that Duff, my first rescued Westie, and Heather came into my life. Wendy represents the Westie Rescue group in our area of Annapolis, Maryland. Her excellent advice and unwavering support helped me ease the two into our family.

I thank my first-draft, preview editor, Larry Miller, and my literary consultants Maggie Davis and Jerry Parker. Thanks for spending your valuable time devoted to this project. I'm so very grateful for your support.

Also a key player in our adoption drama was the capable staff at Greater Annapolis Veterinary Hospital. Wendy is on the staff, and that is how we met many years ago. Since my husband and I moved to this area in the early 80s, my animals have received consistently excellent and compassionate care at this facility.

To the doctors and support staff of GAVH: I thank you for your dedication to the well being of all animals.

Most of all I thank the person who makes my world a meaningful place to be, my patient, loving husband, Robert: You continue to endure our "house under siege" as I work through the transitions of our pack inductees. We live our life together knowing *life is a journey, not a destination,* and we are having one colorful, wonderful adventure. With our little band of gypsies, we set out to face what life brings us, to learn from it, to grow, to make a contribution to it. How splendid to know that we still have the sense of exploration to strike out together on "side trips," such as this adventure with Duff and Heather. I remember when you proposed to me in 1970, saying our life together would never be dull. Indeed. And the journey continues ....

Heather's first day with us ... Duff stays close by.

Contents

Heather Comes Home

Safe at last

She arrived filthy, ragged, frightened, and sadly under-
weight. Her rescue foster parent gave her two sham-
poos to find the Westie coat underneath. Her dew claws
resembled corkscrews. Her nails curled painfully under
the tender pads of her feet. She cowered from people,
shrinking away in trembling fear at the sight of a hand
coming toward her. She mistrusted even the water
dish, worried that danger could come from any direction if she dared let down her guard enough to drink.

Once in the rescue pipeline, this fragile 5-year-old
female West Highland White Terrier found refuge and
peace. She blossomed from the kindness, safety and
love that she found in her new life.

Aka Female Westie

Her name, as she came into the rescue network, was
not Heather. Once I adopted her, I changed her name.
She needed a new name to go with her new life.

In Heather's Garden
Nurture her and she will grow.
Nurture her and she will blossom.
My Heather;
My lovely Scottish bloom.

Heather's new family

About 10 days before Heather came into our lives and joined our happy little tribe, another rescued Westie named Duff found his way into our home and into our hearts. Duff, who was blind, joined me and Bob and our Soft Coated Wheaten Terrier, Indiana Jones.

These new members of our family came on the heels of losing Raider, our beloved blind Yorkshire Terrier, to compounding problems of doggy Alzheimer disease. We weren't planning on bringing another dog into the family this soon. Meeting Duff and Heather was pure chance. Or was it? I believe we were at the right place at the right time. Life may have been less complicated without them, but certainly not as colorful.

It's difficult to separate Heather's story from Duff's. Their lives are intertwined, particularly since only days separate their arrivals. When Duff arrived, I began a journal documenting his assimilation into our family. His story naturally flowed into a book, *Duff at First Sight*, which follows his adventures — often amusing, as he adjusted to us and us to him. He arrived blind with well-advanced cataracts. Now, after surgery, which was nothing less than miraculous, Duff can see. His regained sight leads us to new adventures almost daily.

For those of you who have already read Duff's journey, you will find the beginnings of Heather's story to be much the same as his. Later in this journal, however, you will find more details of Heather's transition, including the many behavioral modification techniques that I used to help her adapt to her new life.

Heather's Adoption Journal

Along with Duff's book, this log of Heather's transition will be used as a fund-raising tool for animal rescue and adoption groups; a way for Duff, Heather, and me to give back something of value to the process that brought us together.

Duff and Heather were older dogs with learned negative behaviors from their past lives. In the safety of our fold, they left their undesirable traits behind and relearned positive ones. Duff and Heather are living, loving proof that **you can teach an old dog new tricks.**

Many people have told me that Duff and Heather are lucky dogs. Sure they're lucky, and I'm lucky too. I'm on the receiving end of the unconditional love that they give so freely.

Rescued pets

The story behind each rescued pet varies, some similar, some unique. Some pets are abused or abandoned. Some are given up for adoption when owners relocate and find they can't take their pets with them. Some pets find their way into the rescue pipeline when their owners can no longer afford the added expense of pets with medical problems.

My rescued Westies represent two extremes on the rescue spectrum, and both would be difficult to place in adoptive homes. Duff, obviously loved and pampered, was unfortunate to have his owners die. He was an older dog, blind from cataracts, and his inside-outside potty skills needed some refreshing.

Heather was on the difficult-to-place list for different reasons. Badly abused, and suffering from malnutrition, she cowered fearfully, viewing every sound and every shadow as a threat. She was afraid to eat. And she was afraid to relieve herself no matter where, outside or in. She was not housebroken, and she had a disease that required lifelong, costly medication.

Duff and Heather were two orphaned pets with opposite backgrounds, both loveable, vulnerable, and needy. It took a surprisingly short time to integrate them into our pack family. They have taken their places in our family community as vital members.

Meeting Heather

On Monday, December 14, as Duff and I were leaving the vet hospital after having more blood work, another rescued Westie entered. Frightened, hunched and cautious, she placed her paws gingerly as she walked. She wobbled as if her fragile legs couldn't support her bony frame. Of course, I wanted to scoop her up in my arms and take her home with me at that very moment. However, reasoning told me to continue to smooth out Duff's entry into our pack before making any more changes in our home life. The little orphan girl was scheduled to stay at the hospital for observation and tooth surgery.

Haunting sadness

Even while I was tending to Duff's needs, I couldn't get the haggard female out of my mind. Her pathetic pose and her profound sadness haunted me. She deserved a chance for a new life away from the miseries that she had suffered. Without a doubt I felt I could provide her with that chance.

I called Wendy, who heads the Westie Rescue group in our area, and voiced my desire to bring the waif into our family. It was certain that because of her daily medical needs she would be difficult to place in a new home. Her expensive medication wasn't the only reason for her hard-to-place status. Her fragile physical condition and psychological problems due to her former abuse all contributed. It seemed as though, through instinct, she had reverted naturally to a wild state for self preservation. Some of that wildness remains with her today.

Heather's adoption profile

She's a 5-year-old female Westie, weighing 10 pounds, and suffering from stress. She exhibits a weakened physical condition, possibly from malnutrition, and shows outward indications of physical abuse: hand shy and constantly wary of her environment. She exhibits a fearful mistrust of people. Additionally, she has Addison's Disease: hypoadrenocorticism, a disease of the adrenal glands. If not treated, the condition can be life threatening. She requires medication twice daily for life.

Currently we must supplement her daily medication with Prednisone until she is no longer under severe stress. Sufficient medication, food and water consumption are necessary to help maintain her body chemistry. We must continue to monitor her behavior for signs of disease. She needs a quiet, safe environment where she will feel confident to eat, drink and sleep in comfort without feeling threatened.

My challenge

I will be able to give Heather the attention she demands. Because I work at home, I have the time to devote to her special needs. She comes tailor-made for our pack family. I've been trained on "medically challenged" critters all my life. I'll pick her up in the morning for a day visit. She'll feel better with us, rather than waiting in the kennel for her scheduled Thursday surgery. And I'll feel better knowing that I contributed in a small way toward helping this forlorn little orphan.

Heather's arrival

Journal entry, Wednesday, December 16: Today I introduce our new little Westie girl into our family. Because of her medical condition, it is important for her to eat. She hasn't eaten sufficiently since her rescue. She is too frightened, and feels threatened at every turn. Bringing her home for the day to a quiet, secure environment might help calm her enough to accept a good meal. My goal for the day is to get her to eat as much as possible. She can stay the whole day. I have to have her back by evening so they can prepare her for her dental surgery the next morning.

I have changed her name to Heather May McKenzie Prince. New life, new name. Heather: to reflect the beautiful, delicate-looking, yet hardy flower that she resembles; it is a light and airy, wispy Scottish name that suites her demeanor. May: to remember my great grandmother. McKenzie: to celebrate our Scottish heritage using my maternal family name.

Welcome, our friend

When I brought Heather home, the boys welcomed her enthusiastically. Indiana Jones (Indi), my 8-year-old Soft Coated Wheaten Terrier, delighted in meeting his new sister. He bounced around her jubilantly. For Duff it was also immediate acceptance.

Heather gradually warmed to her environment. It didn't take long for her to feel the acceptance and the safety of our clan. She followed me closely. Duff followed me closely. They related to one another, bonding instantly. By the end of the day she relaxed, and let herself enjoy her newfound freedom.

Closely monitoring her food intake, remembering today's goal, I tried several goodies to coax her to eat. Her fear of eating is overwhelming. The poor girl is afraid to accept food, even when it is set out away from any activity. She acts as though it's a trap.

Our first feeding today lasted close to two hours. I sat beside her on the floor. She was not intimidated by my presence, rather, she was comforted. I tried tempting her with chicken, cheese, dry food, canned food, even a grape, but nothing interested her. I was perplexed.

Chicken and cheese always, *always* worked with other dogs. I never had a dog that was afraid to eat. And I never had one that refused such delicacies as chicken and cheese.

As I moved about the kitchen putting away my weekly groceries, I looked for something that might interest Heather. Anything. I picked up a container that rattled as I pulled it from the grocery bag. She recognized the sound. She perked up her ears and watched me closely. I wondered, was this a familiar sound of the type of food she liked? What sounds like that? Maybe rice pouring from the box as it was being prepared to steam? It was worth a try. Twenty minutes later, after I was sure the rice was cool enough to eat, I mixed it in with her canned food. Success. She ate about a quarter of a cup from her dish. I considered that a victory.

Again around 4 o'clock she exhibited some interest in food. I gave her a biscuit treat, and she accepted it. We're getting through to her, I thought. Naturally, Duff, my shadow, enjoyed his treat, as well. He is a happy, expressive dog, and very food oriented.

I didn't want to feed Heather too much this close to dinner time because I wanted to give her a good meal right before she had to return to the hospital that evening. I could see she was hungry. Sniffing around Duff's kitchen kennel, she found a couple of pieces of his dry food that must have fallen out. I usually give him a few pieces of dry food as a treat when he enters his little bed. Positive reinforcement. He associates going into the kennel as a good thing. Heather found the food and claimed the delicious pieces for herself. I saw a sign of pleasure in her eyes. As she looked up at me, I was sure I saw her smile.

My heart melted. If she was hungry, then she should eat. No more waiting. The goal was to get food in her, not train her to wait until a designated, official dinner time.

"Right this way, my little pretty," I said as I mixed her steamed rice prepared earlier with her canned food as well as dry food. I sat with her in the cordoned-off safety of the pantry. I also gave the boys their dinners at that time, even though it was earlier than usual. I didn't want any food conflicts. Duff ate in his kitchen kennel, Heather ate in the pantry behind the baby gate, and our benevolent king Indiana Jones ate where he always eats at his feeding station in the kitchen. I reveled in the sound of the three of them eating so peacefully — our little family, happily munching.

The hardest part of that day was giving Heather back to the hospital for her scheduled procedures the next day.

Observation notes

Heather walks gingerly and wobbles on her spindly little legs. She has no muscle. I can feel her chest bones and rib cage when I pick her up. She seems weak and exhausted. The way she carries herself when she walks is sad to watch. She crouches, darting eyes up, down, and around, fearful that something may come from any direction and bring her harm. She is unsure of her steps. It seems as though she never had this type of freedom before.

We will celebrate Heather's little victories when we see them — wagging her tail when Bob comes home, walking on the grass freely with no leash, choosing her own outside potty spots, and the freedom to roam the house, following the pack from area to area.

At the hospital

On Thursday afternoon, December 17, I called the hospital to get a status report on our Heather. Wendy said I'd have to wait until early evening to come for her.

Heather had very bad diarrhea and had two baths today to clean up from it. She was terribly stressed. I had the option of leaving her there overnight so they could monitor the diarrhea, or pick her up after 6 p.m. and take my chances with a messy Westie.

I chose the latter, of course. I was certain Heather would rest more easily at home. I wasn't afraid of a little mess. The diarrhea was a temporary situation, which would soon cease once she was home among us in a calm, no-stress environment.

I remember our now-departed Raider having diarrhea when she boarded at the hospital a few times several years ago after she was totally blind. It was due to stress from a strange and noisy environment. Her little system rebelled. I think our Westie girl is experiencing similar upsets. After coming home Raider's system calmed down in a day or so. Heather's would too. We also have medication to help her. There was no way I was going to leave her in an environment where she felt threatened. She needed calm and quiet surroundings where she could rest and feel secure. Coming home was good medicine.

Picking up Heather
Duff came with me when I drove to the vet to pick up Heather. Poor Heather looked pathetic when the technician brought her to me. Even though she had two baths while she was there, her coat looked greenish brown behind her tail and down her back legs. She was drawn, scared, and helpless. I wrapped her in a towel to prevent leakage caused by her diarrhea and carried her to my pickup with Duff trotting by my side. Heather came home with me and Duff as her escorts. She lay quietly on the seat beside me, entwined in her towel, exhausted and tired of the fight.

Signs of Abuse
Observation notes from first night: Since we know of Heather's former abuse, we expect to find different behavioral patterns in her than those of the other dogs. I closely observe everything she does, hoping to find the trouble spots in her little world so we can help her. My goal is to integrate her into the pack as a happy, healthy, well-adjusted, housebroken Westie. Realistically I know this will take a long time.

Food, water and fear
Eating remains a problem with her. She seems hungry and willing to taste what is before her, but she reacts to the food as if it were alive and threatening. She cowers

and backs away from it. Her fear-filled reactions to the water bowl echo her distrust of even the most basic of her needs. As she creeps up to the water, almost like she's stalking prey, she looks cautiously in every direction, including up. Often she jerks her head upward, fearing an attack from above. Once she's made her approach to the dish, she sniffs over the water, then laps a little, looks around, drinks a little, looks around, and finally drinks her fill. We have deep wounds to heal.

This morning she worked out the problem of breakfast in her own way. I simply sat on the floor and let her play it out. She watched Indi closely and waited until he had finished his meal. When the benevolent king left his dish, she crept, first to sniff, then to take several bites from what remained in his dish. She ate out of his bowl, even though she had ample food in her own. This was basic pack behavior. She waited until the pack leader had his fill, then she took what she needed to survive.

Breakfast
On Saturday, December 19, in the early morning Heather came to me asking for something. I thought maybe it was time to go out. So out we went. Nope. No go. Hungry? Let's try food. I knew she hadn't had a satisfying meal in a long time. To keep the boys out of the picture so there were no distractions, I took her into the pantry, closed the door, and set her untouched breakfast bowl on the floor. Bingo. We have a winner.

Perching on the stairs

Journal notes from later in the morning: I'm cleaning the kitchen, washing dog bowls, etc. Duff lies in the center of the room. Indi guards the entryway. I don't see Heather. Uh, oh. I need to know where she is at all times. She's just getting over diarrhea, so I don't want her anywhere near the rugs. I peek around the corner to see her, ears perked, sitting regally on the third step of the stairway. She seems comfortable and content. She's a delicate vision — dainty and dignified.

Food and stress

This evening at meal time, Heather repeated her fearful dance at her dish. She crept up to it cautiously. I saw her hunger and her desire to eat. The hunger overpowered her fear. She ate one bite, nervously darted away, then cautiously approached the dish again. It's observing behavior like this that makes me wonder if some trauma associated with food caused her to react negatively to it. It is possible that she never had the opportunity to eat her fill without facing stress. And as before, she exhibits the same fear and caution approaching the water dish.

The food and water intake and the elimination process, these basic bodily functions, caused extreme internal conflicts for Heather. Perhaps she was never allowed to eat her fill because "they" didn't want to take her outside often. Perhaps she eliminated inside due to lack of opportunity for outside access. Whatever caused her

She takes naturally to
the snow ... our arctic
fox, Heather.

The dormitory. Indi, our Wheaten, makes the first
choice, and he chooses the smallest bed.

to be so stressed and full of fear had stripped away her dignity. It was my job to give her every opportunity to gain it back.

She's had several accidents here that I discover after the fact. I've caught her in the act once upstairs in my studio. She squatted in the hallway. I recognized the action immediately, and calmly said, "no." Without threatening her, I quickly scooped her up in my arms, midstream, so to speak, and whisked her downstairs, outside, and into the back yard. I didn't scold. I didn't yell. I maintained a positive, cheerful voice, telling her of wonderful things she could discover in our garden as she sniffed for a special place to go. She seemed grateful for that kindness. She knew I wanted to help her. Once outside, she finished the process and received jubilant praise.

She prefers eliminating inside, it seems. Perhaps that's all she knew, for she fears the outside as much as she fears her bowl. She may have been beaten down at every turn. One act led to another reaction, and the cycle was never broken.

Moving On

The positive approach

Here with us Heather is safe, and here we shall break that fearful negative cycle. We break it with love and understanding. And patience, lots of patience. She gets support, guidance, positive words, and plentiful praise in this her new home. We take the positive approach to healing the wounds of old. We'll never understand how and for how long Heather suffered her misfortunes. My mantra: That was then. This is now. Let's move on.

Moving on

Heather's dark past life shadows her every step as she explores her new kingdom. She creeps low to the floor. She looks around as though she's discovering a whole new world, massive spaces that she never knew existed. As she walks, she staggers, regains her step, and moves on. It is possible, from her skittish reactions to ordinary sights and sounds, that she was locked in a cage most of the time. Was she not able to move freely to build strength in her muscles? This possibility would support the housebreaking theory. To keep her from eliminating in the house, they kept her confined, didn't allow her access to fresh abundant water, and didn't give her enough food to fuel her tiny body properly.

We practice cognitive behavioral modification in our little home-based rescue school. We'll never understand the extent of Heather's former troubles. We can't change the past. We can, however, change her future. I continue my chant: That was then. This is now. Let's move on.

The welcoming committee

On Saturday afternoon my husband Bob came home from another week-long business trip. The Indi and Duff Welcoming Committee performed their welcoming ritual to Heather's amusement. The ritual plays something like this: bark, yelp, scream, scream some more, run back and forth, stare at the closed door with tails wagging in anticipation. If there is still time before the kitchen door opens, they repeat this announcement even louder.

Heather delighted in the entertainment. She pranced along with the boys, not at all intimidated by the loud barking and delicious confusion. She proudly participated in the greeting ritual, contributing tiny barks of her own.

When Bob came through the door, he received bouncing greetings from the boys, and a nice surprise from Heather. She boldly approached him and, in all the confusion and racket, rolled over for a quick tummy rub. Three cheers for Heather! She was on the path to recovery, boldly going forward, without even the slightest glance back to her former life of fear.

Sunday breakfast

Our Sunday morning routine remains the same as during the week. Indi is like an alarm clock. Around 6 a.m. he's the first one out of bed. He bows down for a giant yawn combined with long, slow stretch, which seamlessly flows into a whole-dog shake off, ears flap, flap, snap, flap — something like the sound of a rug being shaken outside. I know all too well those sounds are quickly followed by either warm-breath panting by my head or a cold, wet nose in my face. Then it's everybody up, yawn, stretch, downstairs, yard visit, breakfast, yard visit, then back upstairs to rest while the people prepare for a new day.

Socialization

Duff and Heather fell into our home routines comfortably. It was time to extend their socialization to include neighbors who are also dog lovers. Leigh and Mary Anne, who live across the creek from us, were the first to meet the Westies. I took the two dogs into our side yard to await our approaching visitors. Duff saw movement and heard their voices as they came up from the dock. He wagged his tail and barked to welcome these new people into his yard. The barking stopped when I met our visitors at the gate as they entered the garden. Duff ran up to both and greeted them with gusto. Mary Anne brought a pocket full of biscuits for the occasion. Duff knew at once that this was a good thing.

Heather's behavior is consistent in her associations with women and men. She hesitated to greet Mary Anne, but the biscuits were tempting enough to outweigh her fear. She approached cautiously and accepted a treat — a big breakthrough. When she finished that treat, Leigh quietly sat down on the stoop, called Heather over, and offered her another treat. She approached him slowly, cautiously at first, then as if by magic, some sort of light of recognition clicked inside her, and she stepped up to him confidently.

It now seemed obvious, including those observations of last night's greetings with Bob, that she had less fear of men. She's not fearless, just less fearful. Perhaps a woman had been her abuser. We know from her behavior that her fears and her problems, incredibly severe, seem too deep to have been rooted in short-term abusive treatment.

We moved our introduction party inside the house to continue our dog socialization celebration. For most of the duration of the visit we sat on the floor with the dogs. When Indi joined the pack, after the other two had everyone's full attention, all three dogs piled on top of Leigh. And by the end of the visit, Mary Anne had won over Heather with soft words and hugs. Heather sat quietly on her lap to soak up the kindness. It was nice to see both Westies associate so well with our neighbors. The dogs, especially Heather, need to know that the love and security they feel inside our little family pack does indeed transfer to neighboring packs.

Housebreaking

Since Heather's arrival, I've watched her carefully for signs of needing to relieve herself. The Prednisone she was on made her drink water frequently, which, of course, increased her outside visits. She didn't give any signals to tell me that she wanted to go out, at least none that I could understand. I trained our boy Indi to ring the sleigh bells hung on the door when he wanted to go outside. Raider used to run toward me, then flip up on her hind legs and reverse direction. Heather and I had no common language as yet.

Therefore, from housebreaking many puppies successfully in the past, I automatically took the dogs out about every hour and a half to two hours whether they needed to "go potty," or not. Every time I took out Heather, she squatted. Good that I let her out frequently, I thought.

I put her on the puppy schedule. I'd take her out after eating, after waking up from a nap, and every few hours during the day. I also kept her in the same room I was in. I used a baby gate to block off the area when I was working in the kitchen. I wanted Heather and Duff to be where I could see what they were doing. I also did not want our Oriental rugs to become an issue. We didn't need the added stress. Until I knew where we stood in the house training issue for both recruits, it was my plan to keep them contained in one indestructible area with me. If we had any accidents, we'd have them on the worry-free tile floor. That avoided all negative outcomes, which avoided any anxieties in me or the dogs.

Oh, no. Not the rug

Later in the afternoon Heather came to me, telling me she was hungry. I fed her about a fourth cup of canned food to hold her over until dinner time. She ate ravenously, and would have eaten more if I gave it to her. Then I took all the dogs outside. Heather refused to get off the stoop to join the rest of us in the yard. I relaxed my vigil and let her back inside, thinking I'd take her out again in a few minutes.

Too late. She was out of my sight for only a few seconds. When I realized I couldn't see her, I looked over to see her slinking away from the Oriental rug in the sitting area — ears down, tail tucked. Oh, no. Trouble. I ran to the rug, and thankfully, found nothing there. However, just a few inches away on the tile, I saw some very well-formed, freshly deposited feces. At least I had clear confirmation that she was over her diarrhea. And a good thing, at that. I suspect from the close proximity of her droppings, that she had fully intended to deposit it on the soft rug. It seems her feet may have been on the carpet with her tail portion hanging out a little over the tile. Luck was with me.

She knew she did something wrong. And I knew that my reaction was important. I didn't chase after her. I just told her no in a firm voice, then calmly picked her up and took her outside with the boys. I closed the patio door and left them there until I cleaned up her little mess.

Communicating

Because we don't know Heather's past, we can deal only with the present and hope to impact her future in positive ways. She shows signs of undisciplined behavior, confusion, and fear. I must help her repair her self esteem. Then, as she gathers more self confidence, I believe many of her problems will fade. Heather will regain her dignity. It's not a matter of *if*, it's a matter of *when.*

Heather on the move

A few hours later, upstairs in my studio after the "rug incident," Heather lapped up a healthy amount of water. (I have water dishes in every room.) I watched her closely. She walked all around the room, into the studio powder room, then into the hallway open to the laundry room. Searching. She was on the move.

I knew the signs. Puppies start to pace when they

feel the need to eliminate, but aren't sure where to do it. Suddenly, in front of the laundry room door, Heather squatted, albeit ever so briefly. I quickly told her "no," but didn't chase her, as she may have expected. Instead, I ran toward the stairs, calling to Indi and Duff, "Outside! Outside! Let's go outside!." Heather joined in the parade racing down the stairs. I scooped up Duff to carry him downstairs, Indi dashed to the door, and Heather fell in close behind, racing with the pack. She wanted to go out. She wanted to do the right thing.

She ran fast. Ears up. Tail out. Hurry, hurry. Her little legs scampered. Seeing her race out to the far yard with us, squatting well into the grassy area, confirmed my earlier thoughts. This isn't a discipline problem. She doesn't want to be naughty. She doesn't want to eliminate in the house. She just doesn't know how to tell me that she needs to go outside. It's a communication problem.

School's in session

When Heather finished her duties outside, the whole group trotted happily into the house. Heather seemed grateful that she didn't incur my wrath, and that she had the opportunity to go outside. We will work this out. As of that moment, she joined Miss Janet's School of Communication and Socialization. Since she didn't go through the process as a puppy, we'll give her the opportunity to do so now.

Heather will learn that outside is a wonderful place to be when she needs to eliminate. There are great adventures to be had outside. And she will learn how to communicate her needs to me. This will take time. She deserves the chance to get it right.

Rawhide chew sticks and chips

At treat time I separated Indi from the Westies using a low baby gate to block off the kitchen area from the rest of the great room. They can see one another. Indi doesn't feel left out. For his good-boy treat, I gave him his chew stick and he darted to his favorite chewing spot on the entry way rug. I gave Duff a chip to see how he handled it. He snapped it between his teeth and whipped his head quickly from side to side to make sure it was dead — a typical Westie instinctive reaction that I haven't seen exhibited in any of my dogs since Poohkie, our diabetic Westie.

Indi chewed his treat in the entryway, Duff enjoyed his on the kitchen throw rug in front of the sink, and Heather lay in the booth where I placed her after breakfast.

She won't jump up on the seat by herself. I have to offer it to her, then give her a boost. She is capable of getting up there by herself, but she's not sure it's okay to do it. I offered her a rawhide chip. She sniffed it and ignored it. Then I offered her a rawhide chew stick, but she turned away from that, too. Perhaps her teeth still hurt her from her dental surgery. She seems to lack pep, as though she is ill.

I suspect kind treatment is new to her. She's not allowing herself to let down her guard, and is therefore stressed from all the newness. Perhaps she questions how long this kindness will last. I don't know if she has ever had the simple pleasure of playing and romping before. Maybe she doesn't know how to play. We'll keep offering her choices for fun and pleasure as we do for the boys.

Teaching by example

I'm using Indi and Duff as examples to teach Heather. She observes every move we make. She watches Indi as he races to me when I call him. I give him big hugs and loving praise. She sees Duff underfoot receiving happy words and hugs. Their acceptance and praise are consistent. Always happy words. Always positive. Heather now knows that abusive behavior is not part of our pack culture. My dogs feel the love that they are given. And they return that love tenfold. They are happy and secure. Heather understands that she is safe here.

Floor time

Journal entry, Monday, December 21: I'm spending a lot of time on the floor. It's good for Heather to see me, not as some distant giant, but as a care giver, nonthreatening and gentle. Being on her level is appealing to her at this stage.

This morning, while I was on the floor, I called both Indi and Duff for additional hugs and praise, and Heather came to me willingly when I called her, too. This was the first time she did not hesitate, nor did she slink up with her head down, back arched, and tail curled under her. She held her head high. She stepped toward me, confident of the praises she knew were hers. Mindful to not use an overhand motion to reach out to her, because it threatens her, I slowly reached toward her with my palm up, and stroked her under the chin. She closed her eyes and leaned into my hand. I stroked her with both hands, speaking softly, and she allowed herself to trust me with a moment of tenderness and kind words.

Following the pack

Heather readily follows the pack now. This morning's routine was interrupted by an unexpected postal delivery to the front door ... holiday stuff. Indi performed his guard duties as usual. Duff joined in the ruckus even though he wasn't sure what it was all about. He ran barking to a couple of doors until he figured out that the real action was at the front door. My ears rang from the echoes of chaotic madness.

Heather readily joined the chorus, barking, running and growling, following her brothers. She contributed to the guard duties as one of the pack. Watching her as she strutted with her head high, I believed I just witnessed a self-esteem building exercise.

Another opportunity to teach

Heather's confidence training has taken a positive turn. She now follows Duff anywhere he goes. If he explores the pond, she is close by. If he sniffs around the gate, she shadows his activities.

I found a few small fresh feces in my studio this morning. Heather was out of my sight for a few minutes while I dressed, so I did not catch her in the act. I didn't react to it. Rather, I blocked the dogs from the room and quietly cleaned it up, then said in an upbeat voice, "Okay. Let's go out!" Indi charged down the stairs. Duff waited at the head of the stairs for me to pick him up. (His legs are so short that he can't maneuver the stairs.) Once I headed down with Duff, Heather followed close on my heels. Eagerly she raced outside with the boys and headed straight for the far yard and onto the grass.

Giving praise

The three took advantage of their outside time. I praised Heather when she squatted, and she knew she did something good. I called Indi, and he came swiftly. I gave him a huge hug and lots of praise. I called Duff, and made a similar happy fuss. I watched Heather. She wanted hugs too. She approached me, confident that she, too, would receive high praise. She didn't cower or walk hesitantly. She walked with conviction and trust. I gave her praise, just as I did with her brothers. She seems to smile a lot lately.

Small steps to progress

Journal entry, Monday, December 28: Heather's advancements have been so steady, that I stopped making daily entries to her journal. However, I continue to record progress when it is noteworthy.

Mealtime improvements

Heather's food intake increases as she begins to understand that no one is going to attack her while she eats. This morning she ate immediately when I set down her bowl. As she finished the small amount in her dish, I added more. It was a consistent way of showing her that food was plentiful, and that I am there to help her, not to hurt her. I'm gaining her trust more and more. We're inching forward.

A noteworthy incident came as she ate. Indi approached her dish. She growled in a low, confident voice, never moving from her dish. He immediately backed off. Hurray, Heather! Taking charge. She's healing.

Repeat, reinforce, repeat

Around 10 a.m. I took the dogs outside. Heather joined the boys, racing through the open patio door on the heels of Duff. She walked willingly onto the grass, squatted, received high praise, and ran back inside with her brothers. She needs these opportunities for praise to solidify our outdoor routine. Her self-esteem is light years away from when she arrived here on Thursday evening. I know we'll have a few more "potty accidents." She's learning something new and unlearning something old. She's a smart little girl. Her sense of community as a member of our pack is strong. I believe in her. Soon she will believe in herself.

Celebrate the small things

Throughout this day Heather has slowly moved closer to me. Since her brothers hover nearby, her longing to be included in this pack is her motivation. This morning she chose to rest in my studio on a throw rug on the other side of the room. As the day progressed, the distance between me and her resting spots diminished.

Warming to the touch

Another noteworthy achievement in Heather's adjustment period came this afternoon. She approached me of her own volution. I reached over to pet her, and showing that she trusted me, she didn't shy away. I've consistently demonstrated to her that I'm one of the good guys. She acknowledged that reasoning when, after I stroked her chin and neck for a few seconds, she rolled on her back for a belly rub. A belly rub! Jubilation! I wanted to stand up and yell, "Yippie! Heather's joined the pack!" But I didn't want to scare her, now that she showed complete trust. Exposing her belly was not only a sign of submission, but also one of trust. She's been with us for not even one week, and already she's making wonderful progress.

Heather tries to entice her big brother Indi to play with her and the squirrels she recently discovered.

Blooming in the light of love

Positive pack behavior

Journal entry later in the day: Heather's positive action to join the group improves seemingly by the minute. At this very moment, she is curled up on the floor by the edge of my desk, about two feet from my chair. She occupies a strategic position between me and Indi, who lounges on the throw rug in my layout area across the room.

More action. Indi is on the move. As I record this event into my journal, Indi stretches luxuriously, then casually saunters over to greet me, sniffing Heather along the way. Duff, remains content to snooze in his secure cave under my desk. He's claimed that territory as his own. Heather sniffs Indi's nose as he checks her out. He does not feel challenged for his position in the pack. Heather is not alarmed, definitely not stressed as Indi passes and continues confidently to my side. As he receives praises and a few head pats, Heather stretches unhurriedly, and unceremoniously moves to a new location to the area rug about five feet away. Indi, satisfied from this small gesture that he's still in charge, returns to his rug. That is fine for all of us. Heather will be free to come back to be near me any time she wishes — that is, of course, when Indi the benevolent king isn't quite so close.

A "chewie" breakthrough

Journal entry, Tuesday, December 29: While I was pre-paring dinner (for people), well after dog dinner at 5:30, Indi asked for a rawhide chew chip. Duff, of course, wanted whatever I was handing out. I offered one to Heather, too, figuring that she would refuse it, just as she has refused all biscuit treats and rawhide chews since her arrival. This evening, much to my surprise and delight, she accepted the rawhide, plopped down on her belly in the middle of the kitchen floor, and began to lick and chew, obviously satisfied. This was a remarkable breakthrough. She feels secure in her new home, enough to allow herself to enjoy something special.

Tradition and "cookies"

After dinner and before bedtime most evenings we go upstairs to have our nightly grooming session, a routine lovefest before we take our final night-time adventure "outside." Each dog gets a separate time to sit on my lap to be brushed, cuddled, and praised. At the end of each turn, we give treats, little pieces of biscuits as a celebra-tion of a wonderful day together. Tonight Heather ac-cepted a "cookie" treat, her first acceptance. Our fragile little girl is making a transition into our household, slowly accepting the reality that she is loved as a mem-ber of our little tribe. Seeing the expression in her eyes change from sadness to joy is one of the greatest gifts that she could give me.

Westie play

Journal entry, Monday, January 11: At this moment Heather flits and bounces around my studio playing with an old rawhide bone. She ran up to it and pounced on it. This is the first time I've seen her initiate play with one of the toys. She's eaten the chew sticks I've given her, but never gone up to the big partially chewed rawhide bones that Indi leaves around.

Yesterday she initiated play with Duff. Luckily I was there to see it, or I never would have believed it. They both followed me into the guest room, happy to be on the carpet. Heather immediately jumped up and flipped around on her hind legs like Raider used to do. Then she reared up and pounced at Duff ... and growled! He responded the same way. They never touched one another. They danced and teased and made soft growls — Westie play! They kept it up for a long time. I slowly retreated a little to call Bob into the room, but he saw only a few seconds. They didn't want an audience. A friend had stopped by to talk to Bob, and the Westies viewed the stranger with concern. The next time, I'll keep their secret so I can watch them be happy Westies together. I felt so lucky that they trusted me that much that they'd let me in on their play.

Building communication

Now Heather asks me to go outside. She scratches at the French doors in my studio. She feels empowered with that signal because she chose it, and she's used it steadily now. We all head downstairs. Heather runs all the way down the stairs and to the back door. She's so proud that she is the one who asked to go ... and that I responded to her request.

Earlier today, she ran up to me at my desk and barked to get my attention. A bark? No lack of self-esteem there. That was a confident, strong girl, knowing what she wants. She's not afraid of me. She knows I'm there to help her. She wanted to go outside. Of course, out we went.

A special bond

Heather is happy and comfortable enough to enjoy her-self now. She and Duff love to go outside together. There is a special bond between them. They must know they are of the same kind. They love to take their time outside and sniff all the wonderful scents that change by the minute. Scents from squirrels, birds, and all the critters of the night before provide a variety of stories for them to read. I love seeing them together. It's comforting to know that we will all be together for a very long time.

Eye contact

Journal entry, Wednesday, January 13, 1999: Heather continues to bloom. She's feeling more self assured as the days go on. When I walk across the room toward her now, she doesn't panic and run away.

I've been working on eye contact to help Heather realize that I will not harm her as I come near. She still has a wild streak that I mentioned earlier, and will re-treat in a panic if she feels threatened. If I don't make

Heather kisses for me ...

... and for Indi.

eye contact with her and maintain my pace, she stays put and now understands that she isn't my target.

Eye contact is a primal, instinctive communication tool, even in domestic pets. It's basic body language. Alpha wolf initiates it and locks contact with the underling. It's aggressive and predatory. Once the alpha is recognized as Number One, eye contact is the ultimate tool in displaying dominance without lifting a paw.

For Heather, if I don't lock eyes with her on my regular routines around the house, she relaxes and lets me walk close to her, confident that I will not chase her. I maintain my stride, remain upright, and keep on going. Consistent behavior on my part, as I pass her without hostile intent, shows her graphically that she is not my target. I'm going about my daily business without harming her, chasing her, or chastising her in any way.

I also try to maintain slow and fluid movements around her so I won't startle her. In contrast, I can walk up to Indi, stoop over, and give him a big smooch on his nose. He won't budge. He wags his tail, knowing that I'm going about whatever it was that drew me toward him.

Heather watches the other dogs and my interactions with them, all positive examples. We're steady and consistent. Every body movement, every eye contact, every word has an effect on her. Each small example of repeated acts and consistent, positive behavior throughout the day increases her understanding that she is safe here.

Teaching an old dog new tricks

One consistent technique that I use for Heather's re-education is to give her an unending stream of opportunities where she can succeed. "Heather, come," I'll say when we're all going downstairs and she is following me anyway. She gets used to hearing a gentle command as she bounces down the stairs behind me. I also use the terms "upstairs," or "downstairs," to acquaint her with directional cues. That's how I started Indi learning his directional words. "Indi, come … upstairs … good boy." He soon understood the term for the stairs, and the direction in which we were going. After that, I began directional commands in earnest, using his ball games as a learning tool. "Go! Fetch!" on his way to get the ball. And "Come!" with my arms outstretched, using a happy voice, told him to retrieve it and return to me. Indi became accustomed to eagerly running full force to me. Now I can give only hand signals, and he responds beautifully.

I don't expect Heather to respond to hand signals anytime soon. My goal is to have her associate certain spoken commands with tasks, followed by profuse praise for her success. The word "come" is high on the list. She doesn't have a clue what it means. She responds to motion, coming toward me when Indi and Duff race to reach me first.

When I call her to me, and engage direct eye contact with her, she understands that this is my time to communicate with her. Usually when I see her already in motion coming toward me, I say, "Heather, come." It was her idea to come, but when I praise her after I gave the command, she associates the word as a good thing. Going up and down the stairs, using the command "come" puts her in a positive mood, knowing there are always praises when she comes with me, or comes to me.

Heather "potty good"

There is no short cut to "potty training." Training puppies is easier than training older dogs, I believe, because you are starting with a fresh blank slate. No bad habits have taken hold to confuse the pup. There aren't any inner conflicts. There aren't any fears.

An older dog must unlearn bad habits and relearn the good ones. As in Heather's case, she's not only un-learning old habits, she's learning to let go of old fears as well.

She came from an experience of negative reinforce-ment. Nothing was positive about the way she had to face life and live with the fear that engulfed her.

It was important for me to not miss any crucial steps in her housebreaking lessons. I'm detailing those steps throughout this journal to emphasize the importance of using repetition, patience, and positive reinforcement as consistent training tools.

Going outside is now a "plus" for Heather. She asso-ciates good words of praise with the outdoor experience. Repeating the ritual reinforces all that she's learned so far. She receives high praise when she actually elimi-nates outside. I'm careful to be there every time she is outside so I can issue wonderful praises acknowledging her good deeds. I'm sure training her to use the outdoors for her elimination will take a long time. She is five years old with some old habits imprinted on her. Even so, I know that **old dogs can learn new tricks.**

The fears that engulfed her

When she arrived here, she was terrified of the outside yard. She did not engage in comfortable, normal doggy sniffing. I'm sure Heather's mortal fear of going outside was not what her former owner tried to teach her. But the result from the war of indoor elimination was a bad association with going potty anywhere. Inside she was punished. And I'm speculating, of course, but perhaps her former owner, upon discovering Heather's indoor indiscretion, angrily threw her outside to finish her deed. Heather then associated outdoors with fear from her trainer's hostility. Beaten for going inside, she was fearful of going anywhere. All elimination inside or out was bad, placing her in a lose-lose situation. Damned if she did, and damned if she didn't. Yelling at her would not initiate a positive reaction to going outside.

Fine tuning positive reinforcement

Now, here at her adopted home, "outside" is a good thing. I talk to her softly, chanting phrases, such as, "Heather potty good," while she sniffs out her chosen spot. Following her around the yard is sometimes a long vigil, but it's important to be constant with the praise. As she squats, I keep my voice soft and consistent.

She tries to convince her brothers to follow her upstairs ...

"Good, Heather. Potty, good." Once she goes, after the fact, I praise her enthusiastically, "Good. Heather good. What a good girl!" As we head for the door, she trots behind me, proud that she did something truly wonderful. And she has.

Embracing "outside"

Journal entry, Friday, January 22, 1999: Heather is practically housebroken. She's made enormous strides in her discipline mainly because she was motivated. In her early years she may not have had the opportunity to learn peacefully that outdoors was a wonderful place to be. She certainly knows it now. Not only has she warmed up to the idea of eliminating outdoors, she has embraced it with her whole being. I announce "outside," and all three white dogs race toward me as we head for the door. Heather gallops down the steps fast on the heels of Indi and Duff. She barks enthusiastically as they run toward the grass on the far side of the patio. She is jubilant. She squats, receives praise, and feels good about herself.

Final journal entry, April 28, 1999

Heather's appetite is steady, and her weight has increased to 12.5 pounds. Her muscle mass is solid. Her legs are strong. She runs, races, and jumps like a normal, well-adjusted dog. She has a healthy sense of play, and has a sweet sense of humor. She loves to play chase with me. Often in our romps, it's hard to know who is the chased one and who is the chaser. She doesn't play with toys. She prefers one-on-one interactions.

Her coat has thickened to resemble an arctic fox. Likewise her tail is thick, long and soft. It doesn't perk up to the standard Westie flagpole position. Again, like an arctic fox, her tail juts straight out when she runs.

Heather has made good friends with everyone who comes through the door of our home. She's not afraid to meet new people. And she loves to find a kind soul who will sit on the floor with her and rub her belly. If she thinks you need something to do, she'll extend her paw and forcefully claw at your leg until she gets a response to her signal: pet me now, please.

Machine sounds, like the vacuum cleaner and hair dryer, continue to haunt her, but not as violently as when she first came to us. I take the dogs outside to stay in their yard while I run the vacuum cleaner inside. Outside noises, such as leaf blowers and lawn mowers still make her run for the protection of indoors. I don't force anything on her. When she's frightened outside, I immediately let her in. I do believe, however, that she is less uncomfortable with sounds as she settles into her new life.

She loves to sniff outside. She'll walk around the patio, picking up a squirrel or bird scent, and trace it's path. I'm sure she'd love to meet the critters who leave their scents behind. She walks on the stones surrounding the pond, often reaching in to sniff a floating leaf or pond plant.

Duff is her best friend. They are inseparable. As a couple, they are perfectly matched. She is sleek, refined, and dainty. Duff is solid, forceful, and confident in his role as her protector. Where one is, the other is sure to be close at hand.

Our garden grows

It's springtime in our garden. We will grow and thrive together. We can't predict the future, but we can predict our direction, our intent. Our garden is healthy. Its beauty benefits all. We'll bloom independently, all the while knowing that our roots are forever intertwined.

In quest of crafty squirrels ...

... Heather enjoys her favorite outdoor pastime.

Heather then.

Heather now.

We've moved on.

Watching Heather Bloom
A tribute

Heather came to us bearing the scars of a life-long winter.
Her soul knew only sadness.
Her eyes sought refuge from the pain.
The burdens on this fragile flower
fixed her soul in winter's icy bondage.
No escape.
Until spring.
Spring's blossoms
gently
kindly
lovingly opened their petals to offer Heather
a new reality.
In the spring the joy of the sun, the seeds of kindness,
the gentle rains of soul-nurturing devotion
bathed her in promises of renewed life.
Today the breeze whispers songs of celebration
for the rebirth of this gentle, young soul.
The winds sing,
the spirits soar,
the sun blesses her with warmth.
The gods smile
for they know the winter gift they gave us
would extend far beyond our tiny garden.
It's springtime in our garden.
The soft hues of life renewed
fill to overflow.
It's springtime in our garden.
We will grow and thrive together, and all the while
be grateful for the enriching joy of
watching Heather bloom.

jp

Hey, Heather! Wanna play?

Whoppie duuuu!

Promise you won't tell Mom.

Who us? Nah. We're innocent.

Author Profile

Janet McKenzie Prince is a niche-market independent publisher in Annapolis, Maryland. Much of the work she releases under *Burley Creek Studio* is used in fund raising by charitable organizations. On a similar note, to promote environmental awareness, she donates a portion of the profits under her *frog creek annapolis* label to environmental organizations for research, protection, and restoration.

She has a broad professional background, serving at various times as a free-lance writer, a newspaper travel correspondent and photographer in the U.S. as well as in Mexico; and a columnist, photographer and feature writer in Pennsylvania.

Prince shares a home in Annapolis, Maryland with her husband Robert and their three dogs, Indiana Jones, Duff, and Heather. She and her husband have had homes in Connecticut, Great Britain, California, Idaho, Pennsylvania and Mexico City. For three years they lived and traveled throughout Mexico, studying Mayan history, and learning Spanish. There she served as a travel correspondent for *The News*, Mexico's English language newspaper.

With concentrations in the fields of print journalism, publication design and production, she holds a bachelor's degree from The University of Maryland and a master's degree from the University of Baltimore, Yale Gordon College. Additionally, she has studied at California State University at Los Angeles and San Diego, Pasadena City College in California (Associate of Arts), and the Instituto de Idiomas in Mexico City.

Other books by the author
Bienvenido a Mexico! 1977, Gilbert Commonwealth
Day Trips Out of Reading, 1982, Reading Eagle Company
Pennsylvania Highlights, 1984, Reading Eagle Company
How to Discover Berks County, 1985, Reading Eagle Company
New Cooks on the Block, 1992, Cottage of Arts in Annapolis